The Puzzle Peep-show

Naomi Games was born in London into a family of
designers. After studying Graphic Design at the
London College of Printing she worked for many
years as a playleader in a council playcentre —
with children of all ages, backgrounds and
abilities. It was this experience which inspired her
creative and educational approach to play, and in
her work as a freelance designer she has
concentrated on designing for educational and
children's publications. She is especially
interested in puzzle design and has originated
hundreds of puzzles throughout the years for
well-known comics and annuals. *The Puzzle
Peep-show* is her first book.

THE PUZZLE PEEPSHOW

Naomi Games

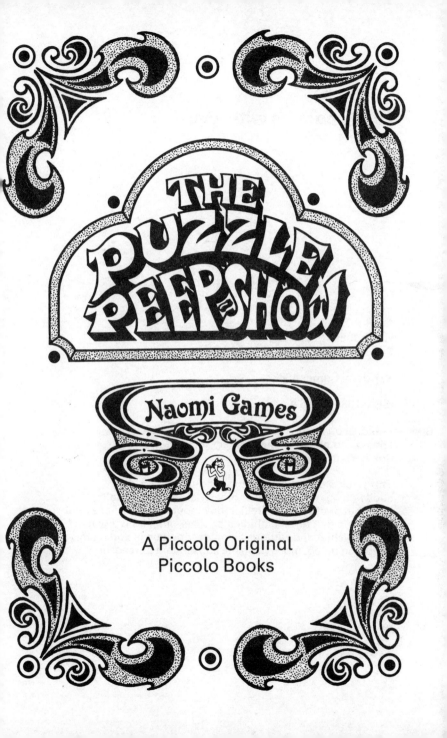

A Piccolo Original
Piccolo Books

To my parents with love

First published 1983 by Pan Books Ltd,
Cavaye Place, London SW10 9PG

© Naomi Games 1983

ISBN 0 330 26996 8

Photoset by Parker Typesetting Service, Leicester
Printed and bound in Great Britain by
Cox & Wyman Ltd, Reading

CONTENTS

NOTES

Now Puzzle Peep-show is your book.
It is for you to take a look,
And for you perhaps to share
With any others who may be near.
Just open up the pages,
The puzzles will take you ages.
You will find that some are easy
But also that some are teasy.
And when the puzzles you perceive
The answers you may not believe!
But if you don't do them all at once
We won't think you are a dunce!
There are lots of things to do,
You can colour in the pages too.
A small, square mirror would be dandy,
Pencils, glue and scissors
  will come in handy.
When you come to the pages
  you may trace or cut,
And then, when finished with,
  the covers shut.
So now here's wishing you
  lots and lots of luck
As into your pocket this book you tuck,
And keep this motto in your brain
Repeating over and over again;
ONE HUNDRED SMILES PER HOUR
WITH PEEP-SHOW PUZZLE POWER!

1. One-Armed Bandit

Fill in the missing objects. There should be one of each in each row, reading down or across.

CLUE: There is a special order in which to do this!

Flick the pages quickly to find out what you can buy at the fair.

2. Helter Skelter

By changing just one letter at a time, turn a cow into a rat, a dog into a cat and a pig into a bat. A new word must be made at each stage.

COW...

...RAT

DOG...

...CAT

PIG...

...BAT

3. Tunnel of Love

Can you find your
way to the small heart
at the centre?

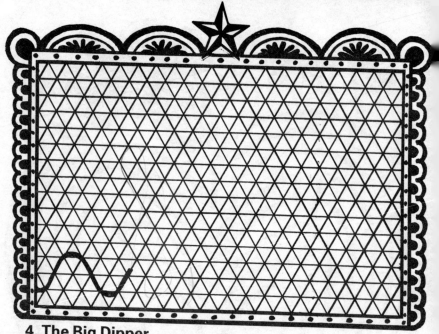

4. The Big Dipper

With the help of the grid, finish drawing your own Big Dipper.

A

B

C

D

E

F

5. Candy Floss

Two of these sticks of candy floss are different from the others. Can you find them?

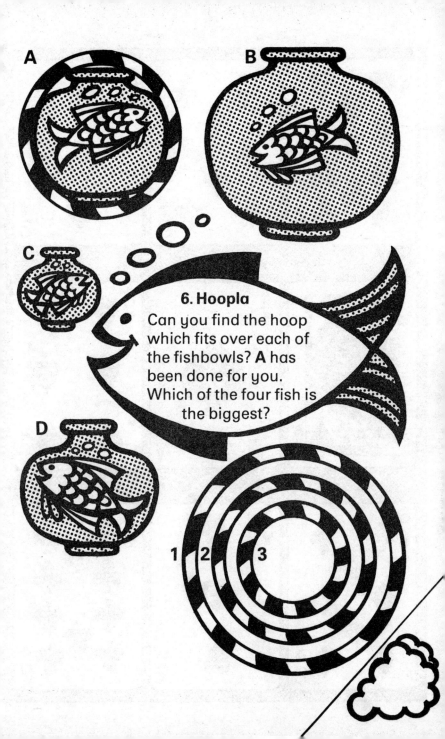

6. Hoopla

Can you find the hoop which fits over each of the fishbowls? **A** has been done for you. Which of the four fish is the biggest?

7. Throw a Dart

There are two mistakes hidden in this pack of cards. Can you find them? Then stand the book up, close your eyes and try to put your finger on the Ace of Spades. Play this with a friend or make up some different rules.

SIDE SHOW

A
B
C
D

E
F
G
H

8. Unscramble the four parts of each of the sideshow entertainers to make The Snake Lady, The Strong Man and The Bearded Lady.

I

J

K

L

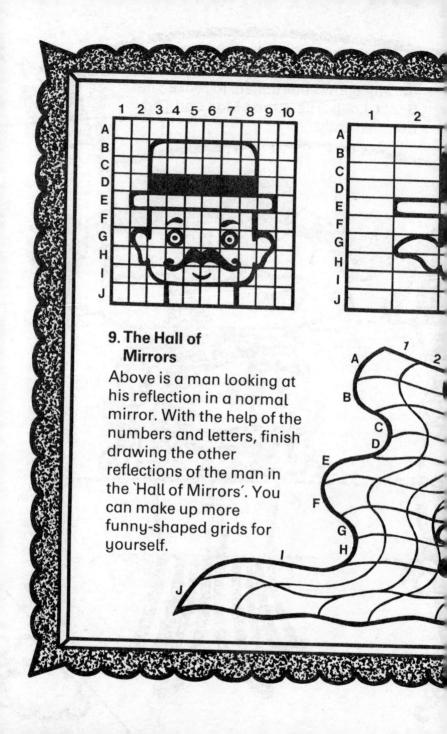

9. The Hall of Mirrors

Above is a man looking at his reflection in a normal mirror. With the help of the numbers and letters, finish drawing the other reflections of the man in the 'Hall of Mirrors'. You can make up more funny-shaped grids for yourself.

10. Punny Food

Name the different foods represented by these four pictures.

11. Spaghetti-Eating Race

Which of the three boys is the winner?
Which bowls belong to the other two boys?

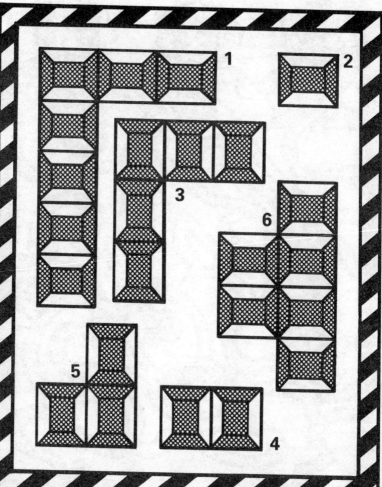

12. Chocolate Puzzle

Some greedy person has broken up this chocolate bar. Try to put it back together (3 pieces across, 8 down). You can trace and cut out the 6 sections if you wish.

almost dried out the wets

13. Fish and Chips

How many chips can you find left on the paper? What type of fish was eaten with the chips? The newspaper will give you the clue.

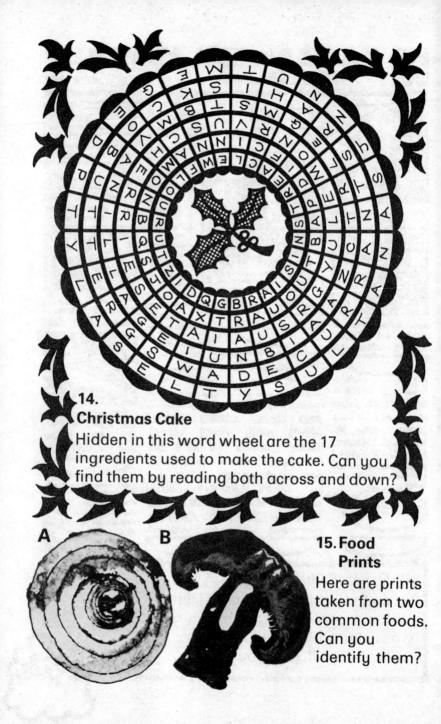

14.
Christmas Cake

Hidden in this word wheel are the 17 ingredients used to make the cake. Can you find them by reading both across and down?

A

B

15. Food Prints

Here are prints taken from two common foods. Can you identify them?

16. Knotty Straws

Which one of these three straws would make a real knot if you pulled both ends?

17. Birthday Cake

Which one of the four slices of cake is the one that was cut from the birthday cake: A, B, C or D?

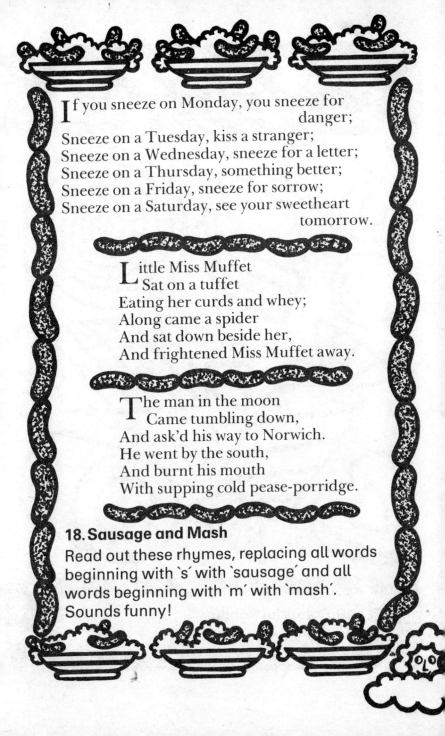

If you sneeze on Monday, you sneeze for
danger;
Sneeze on a Tuesday, kiss a stranger;
Sneeze on a Wednesday, sneeze for a letter;
Sneeze on a Thursday, something better;
Sneeze on a Friday, sneeze for sorrow;
Sneeze on a Saturday, see your sweetheart
tomorrow.

Little Miss Muffet
Sat on a tuffet
Eating her curds and whey;
Along came a spider
And sat down beside her,
And frightened Miss Muffet away.

The man in the moon
Came tumbling down,
And ask'd his way to Norwich.
He went by the south,
And burnt his mouth
With supping cold pease-porridge.

18. Sausage and Mash

Read out these rhymes, replacing all words
beginning with `s´ with `sausage´ and all
words beginning with `m´ with `mash´.
Sounds funny!

19. Colourful Candy
Just colour them in!

OYDRLLU MEOA BH

ESICQ UKS KMI

VYL OIO EU

AYLEG CUF

PIBLUB SEHR RI

20. Love Hearts
Unscramble the letters to find out what messages are on the sweets. The number of words on each heart remains the same.

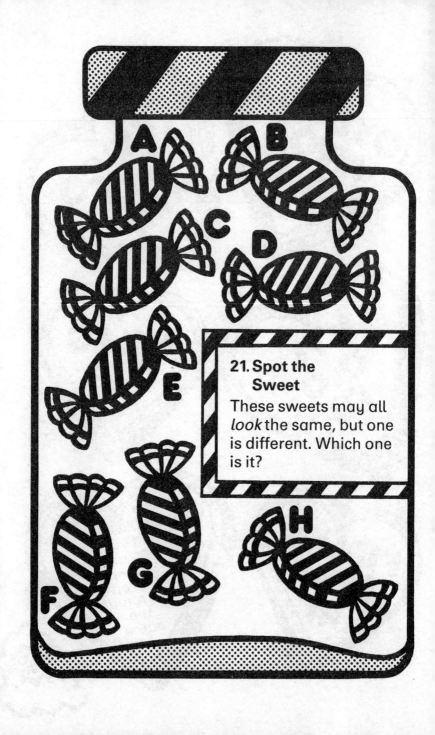

21. Spot the Sweet

These sweets may all *look* the same, but one is different. Which one is it?

22. Count the Sweets

Take a quick look at this page and then try to guess how many sweets are in the jar. No counting!

MIRRORS

23. Mirror Fun
Find a small, straight-edged mirror (double-sided if possible).

Lay its edge along the dotted lines and you will make the clown 'dance' and turn the elephant into a clown!

24. Reflections

Which clown is reflected in the mirror above; **A**, **B** or **C**?

25. Mirror Tricks

Use your mirror to open and close the fan . . .

. . . to change the expression on the clown's face . . .

. . . to make the snake wiggle and change shape . . .

. . . and to make the spy appear and disappear.

26. Mirror Images
Colour in these images. Then use your mirror to make them whole!

Using the mirror, make the cake whole!

Again with the mirror, turn this parcel into a house!

 Lay some paper in front of a mirror. Then, looking only into the mirror, try to draw this envelope without taking your hand off the paper.

L HCPF
YCU ARF
APLF TC
DFCCDF
THF
NFSSAGFS
LN THFS
PCCK.

27. Mirror Message

If you put the edge of your mirror down
or across the centre of *some* of these
letters, this message will make sense!
Can you see which are the trick letters?

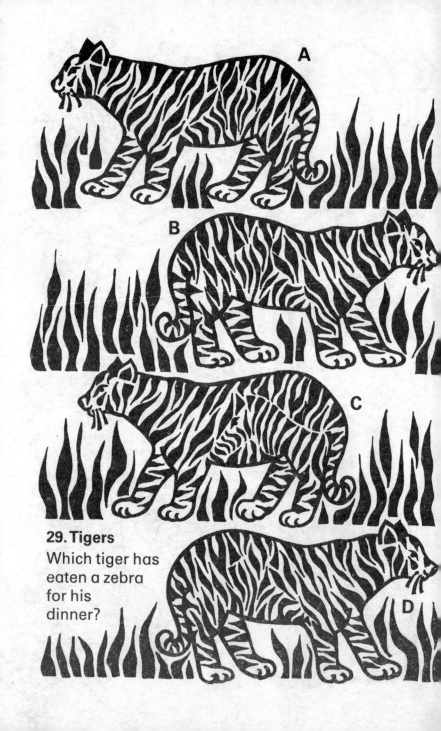

29. Tigers
Which tiger has eaten a zebra for his dinner?

30. Giraffes
Which giraffe has eaten the most apples?

31. Punny Creatures
Name the eight
animals that these
pictures represent.

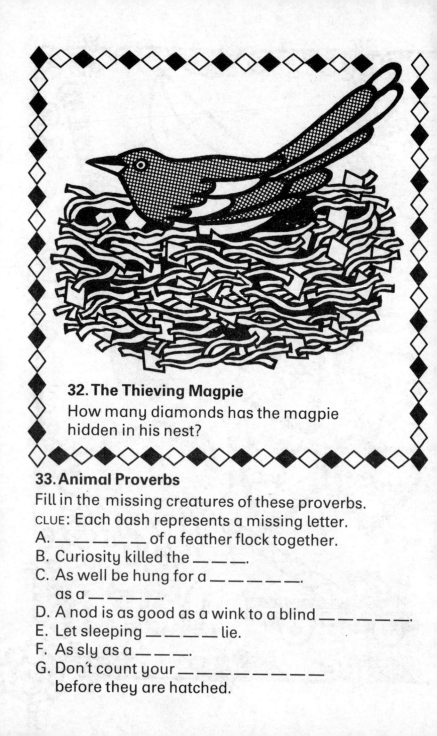

32. The Thieving Magpie
How many diamonds has the magpie
hidden in his nest?

33. Animal Proverbs
Fill in the missing creatures of these proverbs.
CLUE: Each dash represents a missing letter.

A. _ _ _ _ _ of a feather flock together.

B. Curiosity killed the _ _ _.

C. As well be hung for a _ _ _ _ _ _.
   as a _ _ _ _ _.

D. A nod is as good as a wink to a blind _ _ _ _ _.

E. Let sleeping _ _ _ _ _ lie.

F. As sly as a _ _ _.

G. Don't count your _ _ _ _ _ _ _ _ _
   before they are hatched.

34. Creepy Creatures

These 2 animals look a bit strange, don't they? Can you see why?

35. Find the Monster

The two men in the boat are trying
in vain to find the `Loch Ness Monster'.
Can you see where it is? Colour in the picture.

36. Spinning Snake

Trace or copy this snake and mount it on card. Colour it in bright rainbow colours. Then make a hole in the centre and push it on to a pencil. Spin it as fast as you can and watch the colours change.

colour

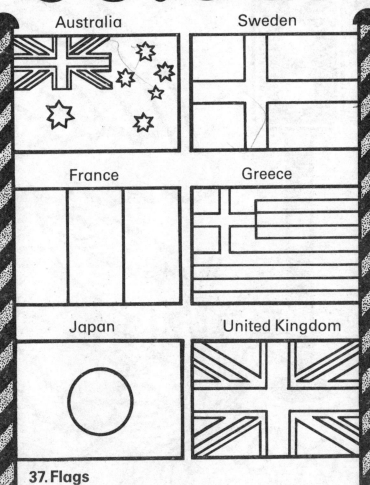

Australia

Sweden

France

Greece

Japan

United Kingdom

37. Flags

Colour in these flags in their correct colours.

CANDY

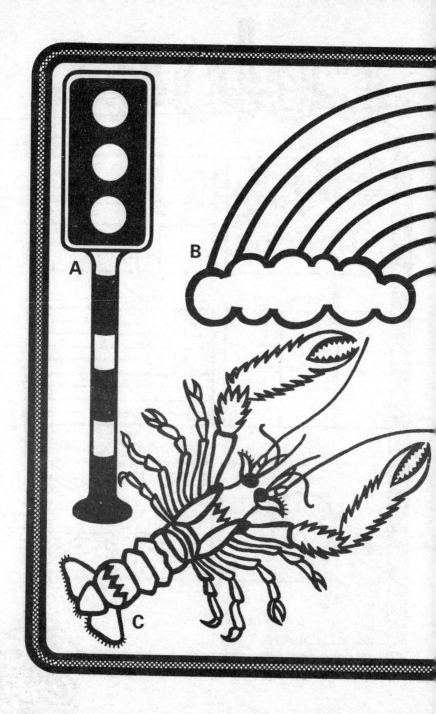

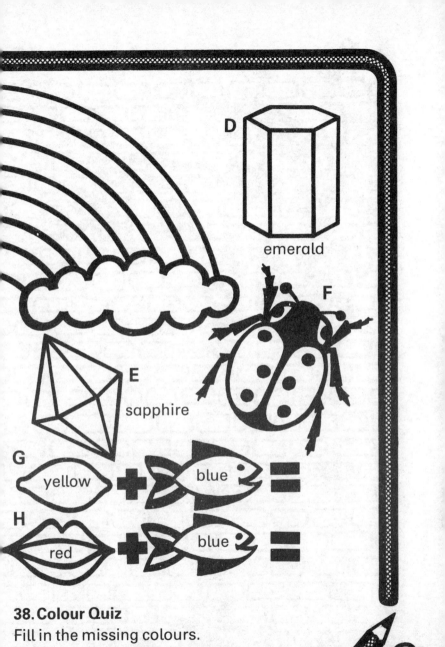

D

emerald

F

E

sapphire

G

yellow $+$ blue $=$

H

red $+$ blue $=$

38. Colour Quiz
Fill in the missing colours.

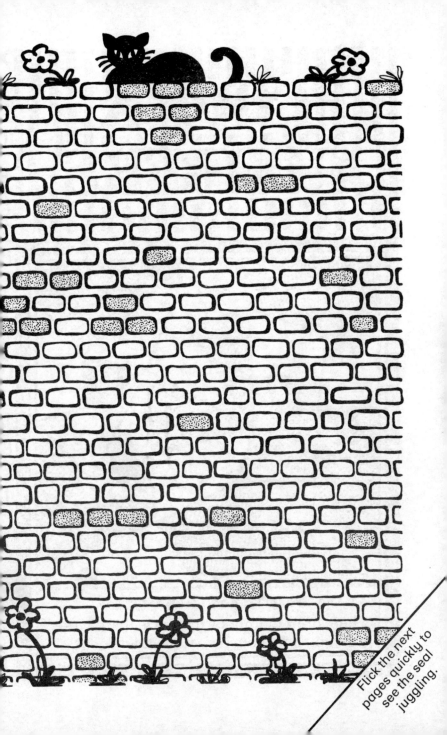

Flick the next pages quickly to see the seal juggling.

COPS & ROBBERS

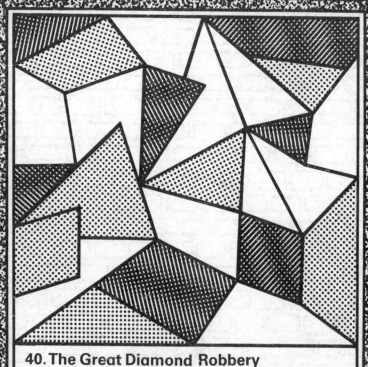

40. The Great Diamond Robbery

There are 2 diamonds hidden in this picture.
Can you find them before the thief does?

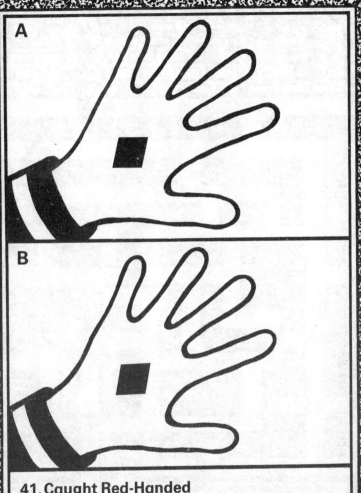

41. Caught Red-Handed

Colour in the background of picture **A** in red. Then, covering up picture **B** with *your* hand, stare at the diamond in the centre of picture **A** for a few minutes. Lift your hand and look quickly at **B**. What do you see?

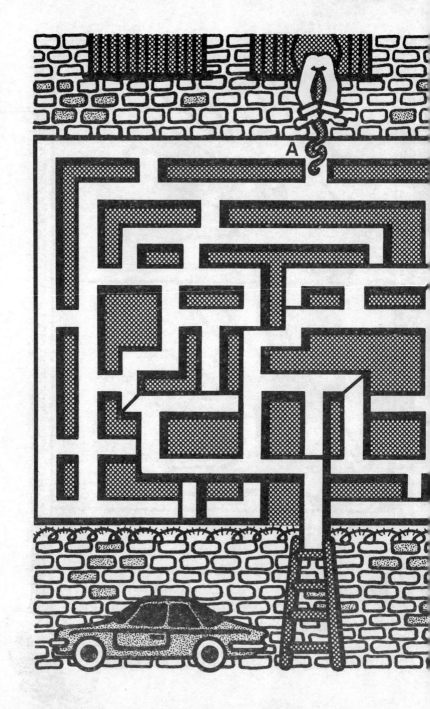

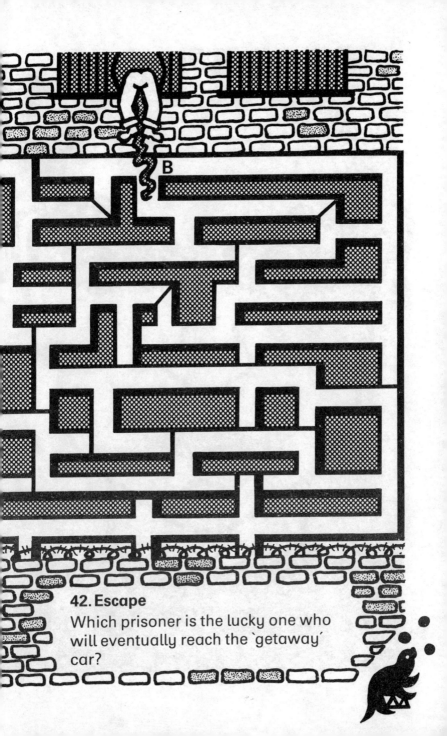

42. Escape

Which prisoner is the lucky one who will eventually reach the 'getaway' car?

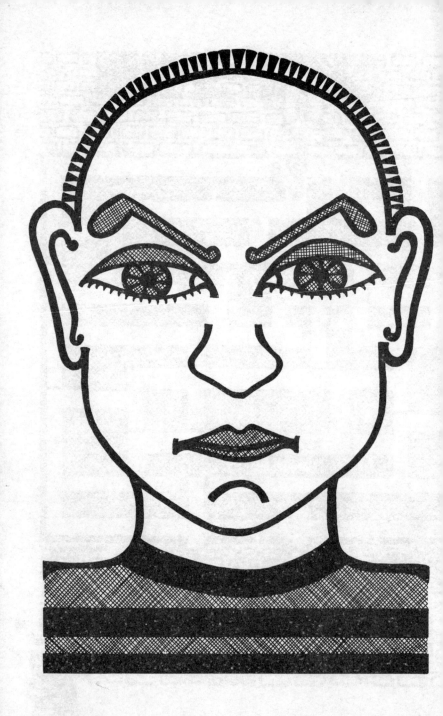

43. Master of Disguise

On the left is a criminal `on the run´. Copy or trace
and cut out the disguise above and fit it over his
face. You can also draw in your own disguise to
change his appearance.

44. The Vanishing Goblet
To `steal` *this* goblet, cover your right eye and,

45. The Getaway Car
This is the car some thieves used to `get away` in. On the right is the same car when it

MOI8 9O7I

holding the book at arm's length, look at *this* goblet with your left eye. The goblet on the left will vanish!

was found by the police. Although the police had a description of the car, the thieves escaped. Do you know why?

IL068IOW

TED
THE 'LOOT
IS 'N THE
BOX
SEE YOU
BACK 'N
CANADA.
MIKE.

46. The Getaway Note
This is a note left by one thief to another after a robbery. Can you decode it? CLUE: Remember another message.

47. Barmy Bars

This is the view from a prisoner's window. He thinks he is seeing things because the bars are not straight. What do you think?

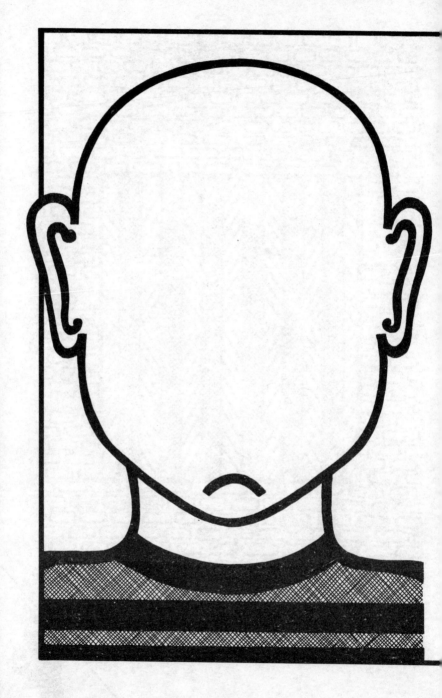

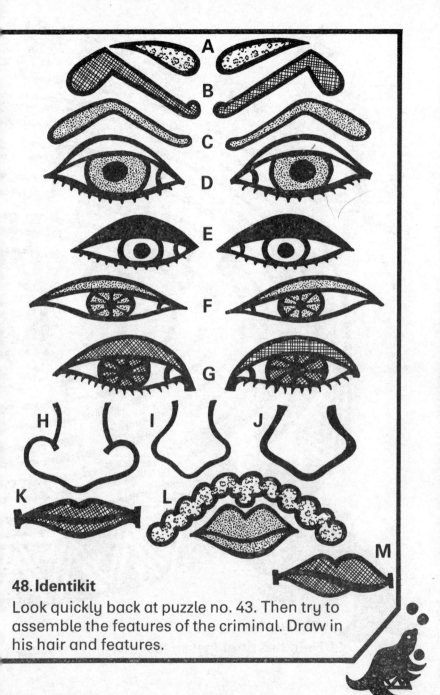

48. Identikit

Look quickly back at puzzle no. 43. Then try to assemble the features of the criminal. Draw in his hair and features.

AT THE

49. Seal Maze
Help this poor lost circus seal find his way

back to his stool at the centre of the circus ring.

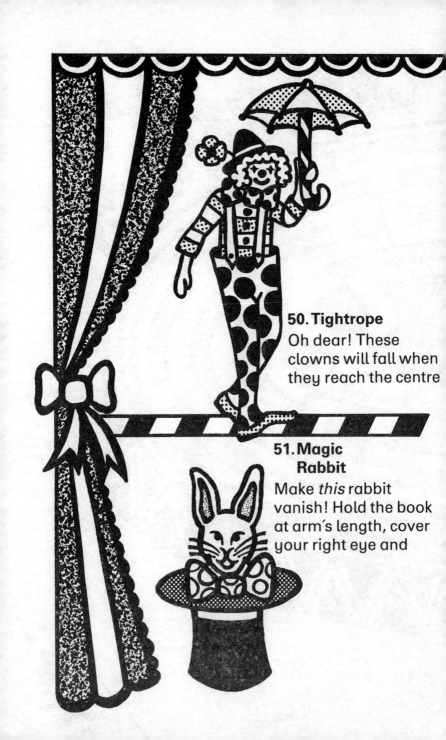

50. Tightrope

Oh dear! These clowns will fall when they reach the centre

51. Magic Rabbit

Make *this* rabbit vanish! Hold the book at arm's length, cover your right eye and

. . . unless you can help them. Can you join up the rope *without* drawing in the missing piece?

. . . look at *this* rabbit with your left eye. The rabbit on the left will vanish!

52. Tall Story

Without measuring first, guess which stiltman is the tallest.

53. Spot the Leopard

These three leopards may *look* the same, but one is different. Which one is it?

54. Juggling Colours

Using good, strong colours, colour the background
in green, and all the balls in yellow. If you like, colour
the rest of the clown in green and yellow too. Then
stare at the black dot in the centre for 20 seconds
and look immediately at a sheet of white paper.
What do you see?

CLOWNING

55. Unscramble the five parts of each clown to make three properly dressed

AROUND...

K

L

M

N

O

clowns. You could trace them, colour
them and then cut them up.

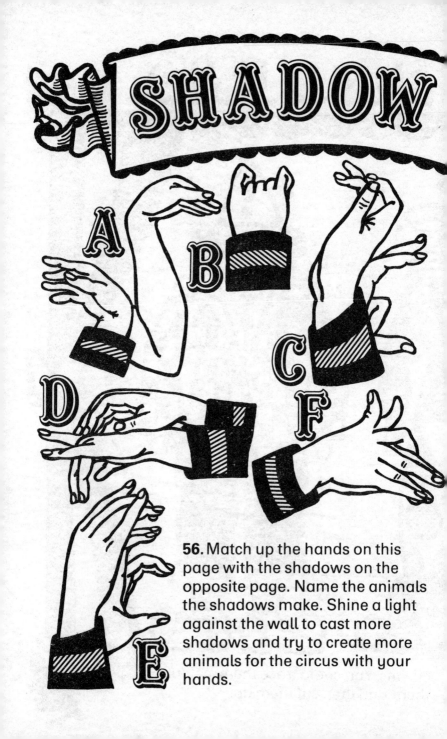

SHADOW

A

B

C

D

F

E

56. Match up the hands on this page with the shadows on the opposite page. Name the animals the shadows make. Shine a light against the wall to cast more shadows and try to create more animals for the circus with your hands.

CIRCUS

1
2
3
4
5
6

AT THE MOVIES

57. Movie Titles

Each of these 9 pictures is a clue to the title of a film.
Can you discover what they are?

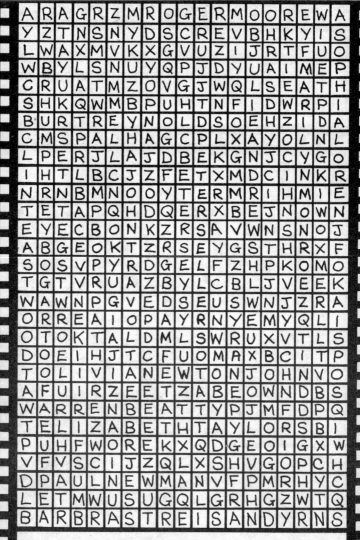

A	R	A	G	R	Z	M	R	O	G	E	R	M	O	O	R	E	W	A
Y	Z	T	N	S	N	Y	D	S	C	R	E	V	B	H	K	Y	I	S
L	W	A	X	M	V	K	X	G	V	U	Z	I	J	R	T	F	U	O
W	B	Y	L	S	N	U	Y	Q	P	J	D	Y	U	A	I	M	E	P
C	R	U	A	T	M	Z	O	V	G	J	W	Q	L	S	E	A	T	H
S	H	K	Q	W	M	B	P	U	H	T	N	F	I	D	W	R	P	I
B	U	R	T	R	E	Y	N	O	L	D	S	O	E	H	Z	I	D	A
C	M	S	P	A	L	H	A	G	C	P	L	X	A	Y	O	L	N	L
L	P	E	R	J	L	A	J	D	B	E	K	G	N	J	C	Y	G	O
I	H	T	L	B	C	J	Z	F	E	T	X	M	D	C	I	N	K	R
N	R	N	B	M	N	O	O	Y	T	E	R	M	R	I	H	M	I	E
T	E	T	A	P	Q	H	D	Q	E	R	X	B	E	J	N	O	W	N
E	Y	E	C	B	O	N	K	Z	R	S	A	V	W	N	S	N	O	J
A	B	G	E	O	K	T	Z	R	S	E	Y	G	S	T	H	R	X	F
S	O	S	V	P	Y	R	D	G	E	L	F	Z	H	P	K	O	M	O
T	G	T	V	R	U	A	Z	B	Y	L	C	B	L	J	V	E	E	K
W	A	W	N	P	G	V	E	D	S	E	U	S	W	N	J	Z	R	A
O	R	R	E	A	I	O	P	A	Y	R	N	Y	E	M	Y	Q	L	I
O	T	O	K	T	A	L	D	M	L	S	W	R	U	X	V	T	L	S
D	O	E	I	H	J	T	C	F	U	O	M	A	X	B	C	I	T	P
T	O	L	I	V	I	A	N	E	W	T	O	N	J	O	H	N	V	O
A	F	U	I	R	Z	E	E	T	Z	A	B	E	O	W	N	D	B	S
W	A	R	R	E	N	B	E	A	T	T	Y	P	J	M	F	D	P	Q
T	E	L	I	Z	A	B	E	T	H	T	A	Y	L	O	R	S	B	I
P	U	H	F	W	O	R	E	K	X	Q	D	G	E	O	I	G	X	W
V	F	V	S	C	I	J	Z	Q	L	X	S	H	V	G	O	P	C	H
D	P	A	U	L	N	E	W	M	A	N	V	F	P	M	R	H	Y	C
L	E	T	M	W	U	S	U	G	Q	L	G	R	H	G	Z	W	T	Q
B	A	R	B	R	A	S	T	R	E	I	S	A	N	D	Y	R	N	S

58. Search for the Stars

By searching both across and down, can
you find the names of 14 famous film actors
and actresses – past and present?

CARRY ON...

A
B
C
D
E
F
G
H

59. Carry On Quizzing
Can you complete the titles of these eight `Carry On' films? Do you know of any others?

60. Comic Quiz
Can you recognize these 5 famous

A

B

C

D

comedians of the cinema? All but one were from the days of the silent movies.

61. JOIN THE DOTS

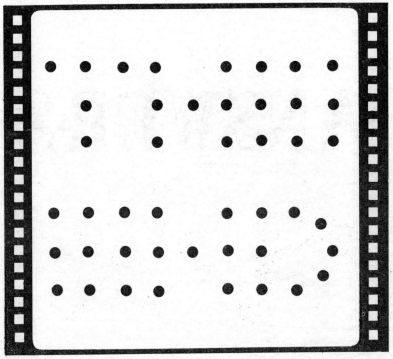

If you join the dots correctly, you will make 2 words.

ANSWERS

1. One-Armed Bandit

2. Helter Skelter
COW-ROW-RAW-RAT
or
COW-COT-CAT-RAT
DOG-DOT-COT-CAT
PIG-BIG-BIT-BAT

3. Tunnel Of Love

5. Candy Floss
C and E are different.

6. Hoopla
B−1, C−3, D−2.
D is the biggest fish.

7. Throw a Dart
10 of hearts
7 of diamonds
are wrong.

8. Sideshow

AJCH = Snake Lady
EBGL = Bearded Lady
IFKD = Strong Man

10. Punny Food

A. Fish Fingers
B. Strawberry `Moose´!
C. Mussels
D. Hot Dog

11. Spaghetti-Eating Race

2–A
3–C
1 is the winner.

12. Chocolate Puzzle

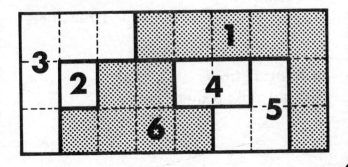

13. Fish and Chips
There are 25 chips.
The fish was `SKATE´.

14. Christmas Cake

1. Dates	10. Cinnamon
2. Brandy	11. Lemon
3. Sugar	12. Vanilla
4. Salt	13. Butter
5. Nuts	14. Currants
6. Eggs	15. Nutmeg
7. Raisins	16. Sultanas
8. Treacle	17. Cherries
9. Flour	

Did you find them all?

15. Food Prints
A. Onion
B. Mushroom
Try some other vegetables and fruit prints!

16. Knotty Straws
B would make a knot if pulled.

17. Birthday Cake
C is the missing slice.

20. Love Hearts

21. Spot the Sweet
A is the different sweet.

22. Count the Sweets
There are 66 sweets in the jar.

24. Reflections
Clown C is reflected in the mirror.

25. Mirror Tricks
To open and close the fan, put the edge of the mirror on one edge of the fan and slowly move it round to the other end, and back again.

To make the snake wiggle and the clown change his expression, just move the edge of your mirror over the pictures in any way you like.

To make the spy appear . . . Lay the edge of the mirror down the centre of the tree. You can see both sides of the spy. You can make him disappear if you turn the mirror the other way up, and lay it in the same position.

26. Mirror Images

Were you baffled by the mountain scene? If you lay the edge of the mirror across the bottom you will see the reflection of the boat, trees and mountain in a lake!

Lay the edge of the mirror down the centre of the cake to make it whole again.

Lay the edge of the mirror down the centre of the parcel, and you will see a house.

27. Mirror Message

I HOPE YOU ARE ABLE TO DECODE THE MESSAGES IN THIS BOOK.

28. SEA-ing Things

A. Star-Fish
B. Jelly-Fish
C. Dog-Fish
D. Octo-Pus(s)
E. Sword-Fish
F. Sea-Horse

29. Tigers
Tiger C has eaten the zebra.

30. Giraffes
Giraffe D has eaten the most apples.

31. Punny Creatures
A. MONK + KEY = Monkey
B. CRICKET
C. CAT + PILLAR = Caterpillar
D. Kingfisher
E. Bat
F. Beatles = Beetles
G. Crane
H. RAIN + DEER = Reindeer

32. The Thieving Magpie
The magpie has 23 diamonds hidden in his nest.

33. Animal Proverbs
A. BIRDS
B. CAT
C. SHEEP as a LAMB
D. HORSE
E. DOGS
F. FOX
G. CHICKENS

34. Creepy Creatures

Animal A has a tail of a zebra, the body of a kangaroo and the head of a lion.

Animal B has the tail of a fish, the body of a giraffe and the head of a rhinoceros.

35. Find the Monster

37. Flags

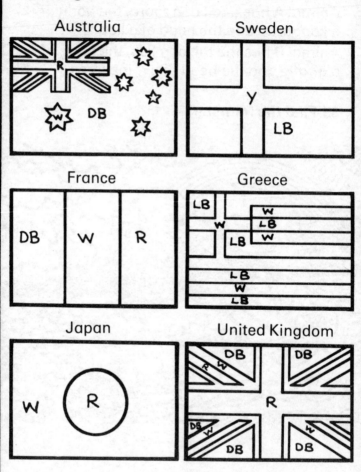

Australia

Sweden

France

Greece

Japan

United Kingdom

Colour key: LB=Light blue, DB=Dark blue, Y=Yellow,
R=Red, O=Orange, V=Violet, I=Indigo, P=Pink,
B=Blue, G=Green, W=White

38. Colour Quiz

A.

B.

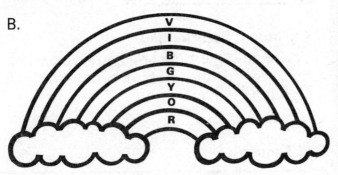

C. A lobster is pink.
D. An emerald is green.
E. A sapphire is blue.
F. A ladybird is red.
G. Yellow and blue = green.
H. Red and blue = purple.

40. The Great Diamond Robbery

Here are the two diamonds.

41. Caught Red-Handed

You should see a red hand against a white background, due to a temporary switch of signals to the brain.

42. Escape

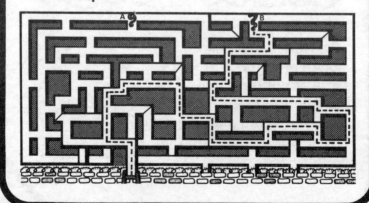

44. The Vanishing Goblet
The goblet will vanish because of a blind spot in all normal vision.

45. The Getaway Car
The police could not find the car because the thieves turned the number plate upside down.

46. Getaway Note
Use your mirror to complete the message!
TED,
THE LOOT IS IN THE BOX.
SEE YOU BACK IN CANADA.
MIKE.

47. Barmy Bars
The bars *are* straight, but they just look crooked because of an optical illusion.

48. Identikit
B, G, J and K are the features of the criminal.

49. Seal Maze

50. Tightrope
If you lift the book slowly towards your nose you will see the tightrope join up.

51. The Magic Rabbit
The explanation is the same as for no. 44.

52. Tall Story
The stiltmen are all the same size.

53. Spot the Leopard
Leopard C is different.

54. Juggling Colours

You should see blue balls against a red (pink) background, because of a temporary switch of signals to your brain.

55. Clowning Around

1. ALHNJ
2. FBMDO
3. KGCIE

56. Shadow Circus

A−3, B−5, C−1, D−2, F−6, E−4.

57. Movie Titles

A. A Fistful of Dollars
B. The Jungle Book
C. Singing in the Rain
D. Star Wars
E. 101 Dalmatians
F. Fiddler on the Roof
G. The Ten Commandments
H. The Red Balloon
I. Diamonds are Forever

58. Search for the Stars
1. Roger Moore
2. Burt Reynolds
3. Olivia Newton-John
4. Warren Beatty
5. Elizabeth Taylor
6. Paul Newman
7. Barbra Streisand
8. Clint Eastwood
9. Humphrey Bogart
10. John Travolta
11. Peter Sellers
12. Julie Andrews
13. Sophia Loren
14. Marilyn Monroe

59. Carry On . . .
A. Camping
B. Cleo (Cleopatra)
C. Sergeant
D. Cowboy
E. Teacher
F. Nurse
G. Doctor
H. Constable

60. Comic Quiz
A. Woody Allen
B. Groucho Marx
C. Charlie Chaplin
D. Laurel and Hardy

61. Join the Dots
THE
END!